BOOK ANALYSIS

Written by Fabienne Gheysens
Translated by Soline de Dorlodot

AF126403

The Ice People

BY RENÉ BARJAVEL

Bright
≡Summaries.com

RENÉ BARJAVEL

FRENCH WRITER AND JOURNALIST

- **Born in Nyons in 1911**
- **Died in Paris in 1985**
- **Notable works:**
  - *Ashes, Ashes* (1943), novel
  - *The Ice People* (1968), novel
  - *The Immortals* (1973), novel

René Barjavel was a French writer and journalist born on 24th January 1911 In Nyons. His most famous works are science-fiction novels: *Ashes, Ashes* (1943), *The Ice People* (1968) and *Future Times Three* (1944). However, he is also the author of essays such as *La Faim du Tigre* and of movie scripts. His work is characterized by philosophical questionings about science, progress, time, humankind and God. He died in 1985.

THE ICE PEOPLE

A SCIENCE-FICTION CLASSIC

- **Genre:** science-fiction novel
- **Reference edition:** Barjavel, R. (2005) *La Nuit des temps*. Paris : Pocket.
- **First edition:** 1968
- **Themes:** immortality, lost city, science, time travel, love

Published in 1968, *The Ice People* was originally intended to be a movie script, but the budget needed to make such a film would have been far too high. The story is as follows: a scientific expedition in the South Pole discovers the ruins of an advanced civilization and a couple asleep under the ice. The scientists manage to wake up the woman, Eléa, who tells them of the last days of the civilization to which she belonged, and of her fight to stay with the man she loved, Païkan. Meanwhile, the whole world awaits the resuscitation of the man she was with, so that he can teach them the advanced science of his country. *The Ice People* is one of Barjavel's best-selling novels and a classic in French science-fiction.

SUMMARY

THE SCIENTIFIC EXPEDITION

The story starts with the words of Dr. Simon, who has returned home after having lost the woman he loved. Chronologically speaking, this speech happens after the main story, which begins afterwards and progresses as described below.

While Simon finishes a mission in Antarctica, an outbreak of measles forces him to accompany a handful of scientists into a French part of the territory, Point 612. There, all the instruments discover lines below the ground that are too perfect to be the product of nature, and the most advanced probe detects ultrasounds. Therefore, Simon and the others go to Paris to ask for complementary equipment, which enables Simon to discover that he is in no hurry to return to civilization. The supervisor of the French mission calls for the help of the international scientific community and the media become interested. The average French family, represented by the Vignonts, remains unmoved.

Back in Antarctica, several scientific bases have been set up: EPI 1, 2 and 3. They start digging in the ground and one of the first discoveries is an exotic bird. A little deeper, they find ruins that fall to dust once they are extracted from the ice. Then, they find sand, and in the middle of this sand, a large golden sphere equipped with a drill. This is where the ultrasound waves comes from. They manage to open the sphere, which is cold inside. Exploration is difficult: one wrong move melts everything in the sphere that isn't pure gold. After having vacuumed off the dust, the scientists discover a second sphere, the Egg.

ELÉA

Simon finds himself face to face with the woman he mentioned at the beginning of the novel. Indeed, in the Egg, a man and a woman wearing masks are bathing in liquid helium, which is kept at absolute zero temperature. Their good state allows the scientists to hope that they will be able to resuscitate them. They decide to begin with the woman, as she seems to be in better condition. When they take her mask off, Simon immediately falls in love with her. She wakes up, but loses consciousness immediately. On her side of the Egg, they find objects that probably belong to her, including a weapon which is soon greatly sought after. The woman finally wakes up and Simon learns her name: Eléa. She cannot eat, until the translator, a super-computer, translates her words: she eats only from the eating-machine.

Once she is somewhat recovered, she asks for someone called Païkan and Simon tells her that she has been sleeping for 900,000 years. She has a nervous breakdown. Once she has calmed down, the scientists ask her questions about the eating-machine; she replies that it runs on universal energy, thanks to the Zoran equation. Her sleeping companion, whom she believes to be Coban, might explain to them how it works.

GONDAWA

While the scientists try to wake up the man they believe to be Coban, Eléa describes her world. The earth was differently inclined; Antarctica used to be Gondawa, one of the two global superpowers, the other being Enisorai, on modern-day America. Thanks to a helmet that can transmit thoughts, Eléa shows the scientists the damage caused by the constant war between the two countries. They discover that the man they believe to be Coban is covered in burns. His knowledge is coveted by the whole world.

Eléa describes her designation, which is the day when she received her key (a kind of ring) and met the man chosen for her by the computer, Païkan. They are a perfect couple. The key allows the obtaining everything in Gondawa and prevents fecundation. Eléa shows her last days with Païkan: war is suddenly declared on the moon and the students protest against it. Mobilization is announced and Eléa is called to the university by Coban. She goes with Païkan, but they are separated. Coban tells her that she has been chosen, along with him, to be the specimens that are going to be concealed in a hideout to avoid the total eradication of the civilization of Gonda.

While the scientists discover writing about the Zoran equations on the walls of the Egg, meaning the equation could be explained without Coban's help, Eléa describes how she tried to escape with Païkan in order to die with her beloved. Without their keys, they were helped by a beggar and managed to reach the surface. However, it was impossible for them to get any further. After they made love for the last time, Païkan knocked Eléa out and brought her to Coban. It is up to the scientists to deduce the rest: Gondawa launched a weapon so destructive on Enisorai that the earth was tilted off its axis.

While Eléa finishes her story, Coban's heart starts beating again, but his lungs are bleeding. Only Eléa's blood is compatible. The whole world waits with baited breath.

THE FINAL CATASTROPHE

After this narration, the scientists, moved, decide to promote universal peace. The Russian scientist Leonova and the American Hoover even intend to marry. Simon, in the face of Eléa's depression, confesses his love for her. She is moved, but rejects his feelings.

While the computer is about to translate the equation of Zoran found on the walls, Hoover, a scientist, notices that the machine has been tampered with: the builder of the Translator, Lukos, plans to kill Coban and offer the primacy of this discovery to an unknown beneficiary. Eléa agrees to give her blood to Coban to wake him up safely. Simon puts on the thought-transmitting helmet used by Eléa in order to determine when Coban will regain consciousness. He then discovers that it was not Coban, but Païkan who had slept besides Eléa for so long. When Simon wants to warn Eléa, he sees that she has poisoned herself, joining Païkan in death. The scientists are forces to leave the base.

All over the world, the students meet in the streets to protest against the political powers that were unable to come to an agreement and save Païkan and Eléa, shouting the 'no' of the Gonda students: "Pao!"

CHARACTER STUDY

SIMON

Tall, slim and with brown hair, Dr. Simon is the narrator of the short chapters in italics which appear chronologically after Eléa's death. He gives the story a pessimistic tone and announces the coming catastrophe.

He came to work in Antarctica without any specific goal, and fell in love with Eléa the moment he laid eyes on her. Contrary to the others, his preoccupations are not really scientific. Above all, his decisions are motivated by Eléa's well-being. His love is sometimes egoistic and his jealousy even leads him to cruelty at times. However, he manages to create a contact: he is the only modern man to whom Eléa pays attention. Nevertheless, he does not manage to convince her to live and focus on the future. He ends up seemingly broken by Eléa's death.

ELÉA

Eléa is a young woman who slept for 900,000 years and has woken up in our time. She tells the scientists of the end of her civilization, but does not care about the modern world. She only cares for her lover, Païkan, whom she believes to be dead. Chosen for her by a computer, he was her soulmate and she refuses to live without him.

Eléa's physical beauty is amply described in the novel: her skin is tanned, her hair is light brown and her eyes are as blue as the night sky, and her body is perfectly proportioned. All the men seem to desire her. Although she was chosen to perpetuate the Gonda race because of her beauty, she is also very smart; she thinks quicker than the modern humans.

The only thing that matters to her is love; she doesn't care about the survival of Gondawa if Païkan is dead.

COBAN

This scientist was the smartest man of Gondawa. He heightens the hunger of the modern powers because he could explain the Zoran equation, which enables the creation of everything from nothing.

Confronted with the scale of the war between Gondawa and Enisorai, he decided to store all the knowledge accumulated by Gondawa in a hideout, as well as two survivors in charge of perpetuating the species. This was not an egoistic desire to save himself: he is a pacifist, and he even suggested that they let Enisorai destroy Gondawa without retaliating, so that at least Enisorai could survive. Faced with the inevitable, the only thing that mattered was the survival of the Gonda knowledge.

PAÏKAN

Païkan is Eléa's lover, ready to do anything to stay with her. But when there seem to be no other possible outcome, he brought her to Coban, to at least ensure her survival. He intended to commit suicide afterwards, but when he failed, he fought Coban in a moment of anger and switched places with the latter. Tall and tanned, he is as handsome as Eléa, with whom he shares a perfect understanding.

LEONOVA AND HOOVER

Leonova is a slim Russian, while Hoover is an overweight American. They are both members of the scientific team in charge of Coban and Eléa's resuscitation. Coming from two nations at war with each other, they forget their differences faced with the catastrophe which wiped Gondawa from the surface of the earth·

THE VIGNONT FAMILY

This ordinary French family observes the progress of the expedition on television. Their reactions are those of the masses: the father remains indifferent, the mother and daughter are moved, and the son revolts and protests in the streets with the other students.

ANALYSIS

A SCIENCE-FICTION NOVEL

The Ice People is considered a science-fiction novel, i.e. a novel which creates, on the basis of known scientific data, a universe that is different from ours. It is worth noting that Barjavel is seen as the pioneer of French science-fiction, because his first books (like *Ashes, Ashes*) were published before the translations of the Anglo-Saxon novels that inspired the French writers. Barjavel called his first books "extraordinary" novels.

The scientific hypotheses on which Barjavel relied are as follows: he invented a computer that is able to simultaneously translate anybody's words, and a "plaser" that can cut through even the hardest matter, making the polar expedition, which is never precisely dated, possible. Then, he imagined a society much more advanced than ours, yet placed it in the past. Simon, in one of his monologues in italics, explains Barjavel's idea: human civilization does not necessarily move forward and it is possible that our golden age lies far behind us.

In *The Ice People*, several themes typical of post-war science-fiction can be found, including the fear that technological progress could lead to a war that is destructive to the whole of mankind. However, other themes are also present in the novel, which makes it very accessible to a readership that is less inclined to science-fiction.

THE MYTH OF THE LOST CITY

The idea of an advanced civilization which disappeared following a natural disaster is not a new theme. It can be drawn back to the myth of Atlantis, as it is described by Plato: this myth postulates the existence of a continent which was submerged in the Atlantic Ocean by the gods to punish its habitants, who belonged to a civilization that was very advanced, yet whose morals were dissolute. Although the imaginary aspect of this myth no longer needs to be pointed out, scientists continue to look for the origins of the myth in reality, for example, a city submerged following an earthquake. Indeed, it is extremely tempting to look in these stories for echoes of the changes undergone by the Earth's relief.

This is what Barjavel does: in his novel, he used the accepted scientific theory, according to which our current continents are the result of a continental drift and a fracture of prehistoric supercontinent, and he placed the country of Gondawa on the former continent Gondwana (this link is rendered obvious by the similarity of sounds). To this, he added a much more controversial theory, namely that of a change in the rotation axis of the Earth, which the novel attributes to the use of the terrifying solar weapon of Gondawa. He then completed this with completely fanciful ideas, such as the idea that black people are of an extraterrestrial origin.

However, Gondawa played the same role for Barjavel as Atlantis did for Plato: it enabled him to imagine what the author viewed as a perfect society. There is no need to look for one's soul mate, the computer does it for you; there is no need to work, money does not exist and everybody lives in equality; finally, the cities of Gondawa live in harmony with nature. However, just like Atlantis, Gondawa has experienced war, which leads us to think that whatever the scientific progress of civilization, its demise will always be due to the nature of mankind.

A TRAGIC LOVE STORY

As much attention is paid to Païkan and Eléa's love story as to the functioning of Gondawa. Theirs is an absolute love, which brings indescribable happiness and sadness. Due to the power of their passion, but also their tragic end, they can be likened to Romeo and Juliet. This is a love that cannot be survived. Moreover, just as Romeo and Juliet were young when they met, the Gondas are depicted as the adolescence of humankind, which would then become decadent, and they have the absolutism of youth. Finally, their tragic death, like that of Romeo and Juliet, could have been avoided: Païkan, like Juliet, has found a way to remain with the one he loves, despite fate being against him, but Eléa, ignorant like Romeo to the stratagem of her lover, commits suicide, thus condemning Païkan to death. This terribly romantic story softens the technical aspect of the novel, which is sometimes overbearing in science-fiction. The sex scenes, candidly described by Eléa, are a way to illustrate the young human's innocence.

A DENUNCIATION OF CONTEMPORARY ISSUES

Although these themes (the tragic love story and the myth of a lost civilization) distance the novel from the science-fiction style, *The Ice People* does share another similarity with many science-fiction novels, namely the use of a futurist environment to discuss contemporary problems. Thus, the arms race between Enisorai and Gondawa reminds us of the arms race between the USSR and the United States during the Cold War. The Cold War also started around the moon, as is the case with the war between Enisorai and Gondawa. Therefore, the reasoning of the Gondawa to build the solar weapon which would practically erase the whole of humanity is the same as the one used by the countries that possess atomic bombs: the aim is not to wage war, but to frighten the enemy so as to be sure that it won't attack. The tragic fate of Enisorai and Gondawa is a warning against the fear of the other which leads powerful nations to arm themselves even more and put the earth in danger. Moreover, the impossibility of the United Nations seeing eye to eye in order to have the whole earth benefit from Coban's knowledge highlights the inner egoism of humankind.

Another point, to which Barjavel himself draws the reader's attention in a footnote, is the anticipation of the student protests of May '68. This is where the only touch of hope of the novel resides: just like the Gonda students rebelled against the governments' decision to wage war, the modern students protest against the arbitrary decisions of the global governments which caused the disappearance of

Eléa and the ruins of Gondawa. It is likely that Barjavel took inspiration from the demonstrations in the United States against the Vietnam War. At the very least, it must be said that the book pays homage to the youth and its thirst for the absolute, as the only way to avoid making the same mistakes over and over again.

NUMEROUS POINTS OF VIEW

The construction of the book also deserves to be discussed. The first chapter, written in italics, is narrated by Simon in the first person after the events have taken place; the following chapter, written in the third person, seems to start the narration of the expedition in chronological order. Therefore, we are confronted with two perspectives: that of Simon, who is entirely focused on Eléa, and one that is apparently neutral and scientific.

However, the progress of the story is regularly interrupted to leave space for the reaction of the people around the globe to the discoveries in Antarctica. This could be a UN meeting to decide to whom the gold from the sphere should belong: including this scene makes sense, as this decision influences the expedition which needs international help. Other scenes, such as the decision of a billionaire to lend his computers, show that humanity is about to leave its egoism aside in order to explore its history. However, the most important reactions are those of the people that have nothing to do with the story. For instance, young people decide to create music from Eléa's heartbeats. More importantly, we follow the Vignont son, from his initial apathy to his revolt in the final pages. Thanks to him, we see how much this discovery affects the whole of humanity and makes it question itself. It is also a way to illustrate the entrance into the era of communication, because even though the internet does not exist in the world Barjavel depicts, information circulates with ease from Antarctica to France. Due to this, there is still hope that humankind will not be able to hide behind indifference where his fellow-man is concerned.

FURTHER REFLECTION

SOME QUESTIONS TO THINK ABOUT...

- Do you think that the attention paid to Eléa's beauty and her relationship with Païkan can be linked to the changes in mindset with regards to the amorous relations during the sixties?
- In your opinion, why does the novel not identify who asked Lukos to sabotage the Translating-machine and kill Coban?
- Compare the feelings of Simon, Païkan and Eléa. Do they love in the same way?
- Love vs. science: compare Eléa's and Coban's reasoning on whether or not to go into hiding. Do you think that Eléa is egoistical? Does Coban have no heart?
- How is Gondawa an ideal society? Are there no elements that contradict that idyllic image?
- What does the marriage of Leonova and Hoover represent? Why are they given more attention than the other scientists of the expedition?
- Compare Païkan and Eléa's story to that of Romeo and Juliet.
- Why are we shown the reactions of the Vignont family?
- What elements in the story can be linked to the context of the sixties?
- What makes this novel a work of science-fiction and what distances the novel from this genre?

We want to hear from you!
Leave a comment on your online library
and share your favourite books on social media!

FURTHER READING

REFERENCE EDITION

- Barjavel, R. (2005) *La Nuit des temps*. Paris: Pocket.